The Way

to

Inner Peace

and Happiness

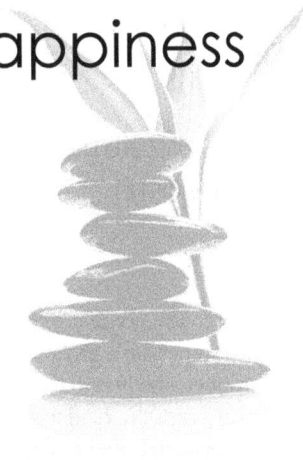

Katherine Helman

ISBN-13: 978-0692305188

ISBN-10: 0692305181

Author's Note: The content of this book is for general instruction only. Each person's physical, emotional, and spiritual condition is unique. The instruction in this book is not intended to replace or interrupt the reader's relationship with a physician or other professional. Please consult your doctor for matters pertaining to your specific health.

I want to express my love and gratitude
to my family and friends who have
positively influenced my life and
supported me on this beautiful journey.

CONTENTS

The Way

to

Inner Peace

and Happiness

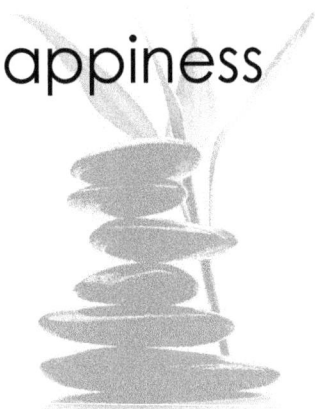

Introduction

How do some people live in a state of peace and calmness, while others struggle relentlessly against the world? How do some people live happily even in the face of adversity while other fret over every mishap in life?

If you examine people who are happy, you'll see a common factor. They are all at peace within themselves. This inner peace is essential for reaching your full potential.

What if you could live the life you've always wanted? This book and The Way will help you find the inner peace that will begin in all for you.

First, let me explain how I found The Way.

When I was 33 years old, I lived in two opposing worlds. On the outside, it looked like I had the perfect life. I was married with two beautiful, healthy young sons. I lived in a sprawling ranch home in an idyllic Connecticut town. It was the kind of town you picture when you think of quintessential

New England villages... white churches lined the main street, musical performers played from the gazebo in the town green, and tourists meandered through antique and craft shops. I had a great paying management job at an up-and-coming computer company. And I drove an Audi – certainly a sign of success, in my own mind.

All looked perfect on the outside. But inside I was miserable. My husband (at the time) struggled with alcohol and this spilled over into our family life. I was trying to be the perfect wife, mother, and professional. I was trying to rise through the economic ranks of the affluent 90s. I was trying to be everything I thought I "should" be. Hell, I was a really intelligent person. I was an "A" student throughout my academic life. I graduated summa cum laude. Wasn't I supposed to be successful? But, nothing felt right. Every day was an internal struggle, feeling out-of-place and out-of-sync with the rest of the world.

And then one day it happened. It was the pivotal moment of my life. I walked into a Walden Bookstore (where I often escaped for hours, perusing the vast selection of romance, cooking, self-help, and business titles) and found a book on the philosophy of Taoism. It completely changed my life.

Now, I was raised a good Catholic girl. I went to church on Sundays and had received the sacraments of baptism, communion and confirmation. I was raising my children in the Catholic faith, too. Reading a book about another religion (or philosophy regarding religion) was not what I had in mind when I entered that book store that fateful day. But as I later learned, God (or universal life force, if you prefer) has a way of leading you to the right place at the right time in order for you to learn and grow, and this was a divine intervention if ever there was one!

The book explained the characteristics of a "Tao" person – a person who followed the teachings of Lao Tzu, a philosopher who lived 2500 years ago. It taught a simpler way of living, in tune with nature, and the natural laws of the universe. Suddenly I realized that I had always been a "Tao" person without even knowing! Throughout my life, whenever I lived in connection with the universe, I felt at my best. I felt at peace. I felt whole. But, living in the way that made me feel best did not match the fast-paced, get-ahead material world that I actually lived in. Ah-ha! So that was the dichotomy with which I had always struggled! So that was why I always felt out of place in the world. So that was why I was always so torn, so unhappy!

My life changed right there and then. I began to educate myself on teachings that were referred to as "new age" – ironic because these teachings originated thousands of years ago! Over the next two decades I studied the philosophies and religious teachings of Christianity, Buddhism, Hinduism, Gnosticism, and others. I studied astrology, energy work, and classic self-help books such as The Master Key System by Charles F. Haanel, Think and Grow Rich by Napoleon Hill, the prolific essays of Neville Goddard, and many others. I absorbed what felt was right for me personally and discarded that which did not.

As a result of this research, as a result of over twenty years of living the theories and philosophies I had studied, as a result of "going within" to connect with universal spirit, I came to know "The Way." The Way will see you through the challenges of our world. The Way will give you inner peace. The Way will create a foundation for happiness. The Way will allow you to make a positive impact in the world and with everyone in it.

Chapter One:
The Way

"Nothing can bring you peace but yourself."
- Ralph Waldo Emerson

So what is The Way? The Way is a choice in how you live your life. It is living life with a keen awareness of what you are doing, how it is affecting others, and how it feels deep inside your soul or True Self. Rather than going through life blindly scurrying from thought to thought, action to action, being a slave to toil and circumstance, The Way allows you to live more fully, more wholly. You live in the present moment, intentionally choosing positive action and thoughts. You live from your heart. You live with purpose. You live being true to your True Self. You live with inner peace, thereby creating your own happiness.

The Way is an intentional approach to life. It is holistic living. It is living with conscious awareness of our connection to the world, knowing that everything in life is energy and all energy is connected.

Living in cooperation with the universe, instead of always fighting against it, allows you to live more serenely. You find peace when you live from the heart.

In order to enter into this peaceful way of living, however, you must first discover your True Self. It is your True Self that has always known The Way and is eager to live The Way. The Way of cooperation with the universe. The Way of complete inner peace.

Chapter Two:

Who Are You... Really?

Who are you... really? In order to answer this deeply existential question, it's much easier to start with a simple one:

What do you believe happens to you when you die?

If you're like most people in this world, you believe that your spirit leaves your body and enters Heaven or some other spiritual realm, while your body remains on Earth to be either buried or cremated.

Wouldn't it be true then, that this spirit that continues to live on in an unseen world lives within you right now? In your body, yet separate from it, the part of you that will leave this world when our physical body dies? This eternal spirit – your soul -- is your True Self. It is this eternal inner spirit which must be discovered in order to follow The Way to inner peace.

Spirit vs the Physical World

The physical world is the world in which you live, work, play, fight, stress, and worry. It is the outer tangible world in which your body lives, in which your spirit has agreed to be born in order to serve some higher purpose (a purpose which most of us spend all of our lives trying to discover). What happens to you in the physical world is often beyond your control. While shopping at a store you might encounter someone who's having a really miserable day – and who shares their not-so-good mood with you in terms of a rude gesture or comment. A car pulls out in front of you in traffic, nearly running you off the road. The computer gets a virus and destroys all of your yet-to-be-backed-up data.

These are events of the physical world.

These are events that are beyond your control. How you react to them, however, is within your control. In finding your True Self, in following The Way, you can face these outside events in ways that keep you sane, peaceful, happy and serene.

Connecting to Your True Self

Who are you, really? Who is your True Self?

As humans living in our physical world, we try to define our True Selves through aspects of our material lives. But, don't be fooled. You are not going to find your True Self anywhere in the material world. It is not the house you live in. Not the car you drive. It is not your profession, nor the size of your bank account. Your True Self is much deeper than that, much purer than that, much simpler than that.

When you were born, long before the physical world could influence you, you were at your purest form. You took with you into this earthbound world all the qualities, values, and knowledge of your Eternal Spirit, your

True Self. This is the true you.

So how do you know when you are living in accordance with your True Self? You'll know because you will feel totally at peace. You'll know because at that moment you will feel as though you are one with the world, in sync with some unseen force, the Collective Consciousness, God. Somehow you feel complete and connected. That is your True Self.

A good way to get in touch with your True Self is to remove yourself from the outside world for a short while and get quiet inside so that you may listen to your inner spirit, which is also your inner guidance. We all have this inner guidance – some call God – and it is available to you at any time when you can still your mind.

"Be still and know that I am God."

Removing yourself from the outside world in order to connect to your True Self is not always easy – especially when you are new to this concept. To connect with your True Self, you need to escape the confines of the physical world. You need to remove all distractions to return to the inner you. You need to center yourself. You need to look inward.

Tuning Out to Tune In

There are several ways of "tuning out" that I have found to be useful when "tuning in" to my True Self. With all of these ways, the key is to get into a "zone" that allows you to temporarily block out the world.

Meditation

My favorite practice of all is meditation. It is said that every great human in history spent time in meditation every day. You can meditate anywhere, in durations from just a few seconds to much longer.

If you are new to meditation, don't be scared or intimidated by the thought of sitting in a lotus position, burning incense, uttering "om." It is much simpler than that. Whereas praying is talking to God, meditation is listening to God. And you don't need to contort yourself into a pretzel to hear God.

To meditate, first find a quiet place where there will be no distractions. Sit in a chair, close your eyes, and clear your mind of any chatter. Empty your mind. Now listen to your breath. In and out, inhale and exhale, listening to your breath with no other thought taking up space in your consciousness. Do this for a few seconds. Congratulations, you have just meditated!

Now, of course, the more you practice this, the longer you will be able to stay in this meditative state. The longer you are in this meditative state, the greater connection you will feel with your True Self. You will find your inner guidance there in that quiet state. You will find answers to questions. You will hear God's messages and find inspiration through thoughts or words that seem to pop into your head yet come from "elsewhere." In this quiet state, be aware of these messages. Be open to them. Listen to them. They will lead you to inner peace.

Yoga or Tai Chi

Can't sit still long enough to meditate?

Try one of the moving meditation practices of yoga or tai chi! With yoga and tai chi, you move, balance and stretch your body into poses while keeping your mind centered and focused in the present. Focusing on your rhythmic breathing and being fully in the present moment helps you tune out the rest of the world and get in touch with your True Self.

Running or Walking

Have you heard the term "runner's high?" It's that point while running where the mind becomes so clear that you've almost lost touch with your body. Your breathing is rhythmic (yes, like yoga or meditation), and the rest of the world has disappeared. At that point, runners often feel completely at peace. Worries cease and they are one with the universe. Running is a great way to get in touch with your True Self.

Likewise, taking a walk in nature will connect you with your inner spirit, your True Self. Away from the bustle of daily life, surrounded by fresh air and nature at its purest, all thoughts released, you can hear your spirit. You are given answers. You are at peace. The next time you are feeling stress, anxiety, or restlessness, go to the park and take a walk. In the walking silence and openness of nature, your True Self has an opportunity to reveal itself.

Creative Outlets

Do you enjoy sewing, painting, taking photographs of nature, gardening in your yard, or any other creative passion? If so, chances are that what you really enjoy most is the complete mental focus induced by the creative outlet. Again, it's getting into a "zone" where the rest of the physical world disappears for a short time, and your mind is free not to think. Or at least, only think about the specific task at hand, while quieting all the other thought clutter. Your mind is quiet, your spirit soars. Yes, your inner spirit. Your True Self.

As you can see, there is one underlying theme in all the "tuning in" practices above. The one thing they have in common is the release of thoughts, the quieting of the mind, the sense of just "being." It is in this "being" that you will find your True Self.

Chapter Three:
It All Starts Within

Now that you are practicing ways to be in tune with your True Self, it's time to start living The Way. Living The Way begins within you. Inner peace is found through your own behaviors, actions and thoughts. Living The Way and finding inner peace requires you to live authentically, honestly, with integrity, without worry and fear, and with gratitude.

Living Authentically

In order to live with inner peace, you have to live in a way that is in alignment with your True Self, your Authentic Self. Inner peace cannot exist when deep down inside you are not happy or comfortable with the way you are living your life. You know subconsciously who you really are. It's the spiritual you who came to this life, and now lives within your body, within your world. It's very likely, however, that the true you -- your Authentic Self -- has been pushed deep down within you in order to make it through your world. It's very likely that along the way, through the circumstances you were faced with or interactions with others, you picked up ways of thinking, ways of acting, ways of believing that are not who you really are.

Perhaps your parents had beliefs about others and voiced those opinions. It's very likely that you also carry those beliefs. We tend to grow into what we know. If you know poverty, you may have become accustomed to poverty – but that is not your Authentic Self. If you grew up with abuse, you may have learned to both accept and behave in abusive ways – but that is not your Authentic Self. Perhaps you were berated and made to believe that you lack worth – but that is not your Authentic Self.

Here is a question: *Do you like yourself?* Someone living with inner peace lives authentically and likes themselves just as they are.

How will you know that you are living authentically? Listen to your gut feelings. The brain and the gut are closely connected through the sympathetic nervous system. Anger, anxiety and other emotions will trigger feelings in your gut. Listening to your gut feelings will truly let know when something feels right or something feels wrong. If you are doing something or thinking about something and it makes you feel uneasy, chances are that it is not in alignment with your True Self. If however, you feel at peace and content with your actions and thoughts, then you are living in accordance with your Authentic Self.

To live with inner peace, you must know yourself and learn to be comfortable with yourself -- even if it does not meet society's, your family's or your friends' opinion of who you should be.

Does it really matter what other people think? Learn to respect your individuality, love your individuality. When you are completely accepting of who you are, when you are living your life with authenticity, then you are being true to yourself. And inner peace will follow.

Living Honestly

You cannot live with inner peace if you are not honest. It's as simple as that.

Being dishonest is like cheating your heart. If you're telling lies, exaggerating, cheating and deceiving others, you know deep down in your heart exactly what you're doing and it doesn't feel right to your True Self. Living dishonestly is a burden carried around in the physical world – it does not exist or resonate in the universal spiritual world. You may try to justify any wrong-doing or wrong-speaking with your brain -- "yes, that person deserved it," or "it's just a small lie but it'll help me get what I want" -- but in your heart, in your soul, you know it is not the truth, it is not right. And it will slowly eat at your inner peace.

All of life is connected through one universal energy force. And as such, what you put out to the world eventually comes back to you. If you are acting or speaking with dishonesty, you will find yourself being cheated and lied to also. But if you live honestly, you can see the truth in all things.

People who live with inner peace have a clear conscience. Lying, cheating, and living dishonestly just don't feel right to them. It doesn't ring true to their inner spirit. And so they don't.

Living with Integrity

Similar to living honestly, living with integrity brings about inner peace.

What is integrity? It's adhering to a high moral standard. It's having and living with moral character. It's being the complete, perfect soul in which you were born into this life. If you want to live with inner peace, you have to live with integrity.

When you live with integrity, you step up to the plate and do the right thing, even when it's not popular. Why? Because it is the right thing to do. Your heart knows right from wrong, and following wrong thinking and wrong action disturbs your peace. The most honored, the most loved leaders – such as Mahatma Ghandi, Mother Teresa, Nelson Mandela – lived with integrity. They didn't do the popular thing, follow popular thought.

They did what was right. They lived with integrity. They lived with inner peace.

When you live with integrity, you do your best at all times. Peace is an inside job. It starts within. And what better way to have peace of mind and peace of heart, than to know in your heart that you did your very best? What if you do your best and you still don't get that job, that pay raise, that recognition you've been wanting? Doing your best doesn't guarantee success every time. But, when you do your best, you know in your heart that you didn't let yourself down; that you gave it your all despite the outcome; that you didn't cheat yourself due to laziness and complacency. That alone will bring you inner peace.

"Peace is an inside job."

Doing your best gives you a satisfaction that you couldn't try any harder. That you gave it your all. That you did what you could, without regret. Doing your best is crucial for peace and happiness.

Living Without Fear and Worry

*"Fear is only as deep
as the mind allows."*
– Japanese Proverb

The law of attraction states that what you think about, you bring about. What you focus on, you manifest in your life. This is a universal law – it works always, whether you realize it or not, whether you think about good things or bad things. So, what you focus on is important if you want to live your life with inner peace.

If you spend your days worrying about things that you fear, you will find that those things are drawn to you despite your worrying. In reality, you are creating a self-fulfilling prophecy.

Kathy was terrified of snakes. She watched for them whenever she walked in her yard, at the park, everywhere. One day while kayaking with a group of friends – and, of course, being on the lookout for her nemesis snakes -- she spotted one skimming along the water. Then, at the end of the kayaking trip, when she stepped out onto the shore, another snake went slithering by. Her friend exclaimed, "How is that possible? I've been kayaking on this creek for years and have never once seen a snake. On your first trip here, you see two!"

The law of attraction. Kathy feared and worried about snakes so much, that two entered her life in just one afternoon.

People who live with inner peace know that fear and worrying do not solve anything. Fear is a man-made concept – it is only something we create in our minds. And, worry does not stop the thing feared from happening. It only makes you miserable, wasting your precious time, energy and peace of mind. Ultimately, it draws that very thing to you anyway.

Living without fear and worry does not mean that you live carelessly, throwing caution to the wind, however. What it does mean is that you survey the situation, you plan the best possible solution for addressing the situation, you follow through with that plan, and then you leave the rest up to the universal forces. Things always happen as they are supposed to, at their own time.

Anita was just completing her college studies to be a nurse practitioner. The topic of her final dissertation was "concussions," a serious condition about which she had to learn intimately in order to write her paper. She had just finished writing the report and was pulling the electrical cord of her computer. The plug was stuck, so she pulled harder, the plug set free and she went tumbling back and hit her head on the desk. Ironically, she received a severe concussion-- so severe that she spent the next several months with intense headaches, dizziness, nausea, sensitivity to light and sound, and the inability to concentration. She was scheduled to take her nurse practitioner licensing exam, but there was no way she could study or even look at a computer screen. She started to worry because she needed to take the exam in order to get a job in her new field, and money had been tight while going to college and living in Boston. Her mother told her not to worry – things would happen as they were intended. So, she set up a plan to get better – getting a CT scan, visiting a specialist, and even receiving acupuncture. She focused on a good outcome, and did not worry about things that were out of her control. Four months later, Anita not only felt well enough to take the exam and pass it, but she was offer two amazing job opportunities that would not have been available four months prior. The universe had created a delay in timing so that she would be available for the right job at the right time.

Negative things are going to happen in life once in awhile. There's not much you can do about that. But how you react to those events is your choice. You can fret and worry and make yourself miserable. Or, you can focus on best possible outcome. You can create an inner peace despite the situation. It's up to you.

Living with Gratitude

The universe has a cyclical nature. What you plant, you harvest (ie. you reap what you sow). What you give away, you get back multiplied, as the Bible states.

Unless you give thanks for what you have, you cannot receive more. Being grateful is acknowledging all the gifts in your life. It is saying to God and the universe, "I am aware of the goodness in my life, and am appreciative of it." When you recognize how blessed you are, you become even more blessed.

The Bible teaches this lesson in the statement, "To those who have, they shall be given more. But to those who have not, even the little they have shall be taken from them." This is not God punishing the poor and downtrodden. It is saying that when you recognize the gifts you have (being grateful), then you will receive more. But, if you do not recognize your gifts – if you neglect to give thanks for them – you will see those gifts disappear. In fact, they have already disappeared because you were never aware of them to begin with.

Sally had been married for many years. While she loved her husband, the way in which wives are obligated to do, she no longer appreciated him. Their marriage wasn't perfect, but it wasn't bad either. It had just grown stale. As he felt her love diminish, he stopped doing the small things (gifts) like bringing her flowers and helping around the house. Now she had even less to appreciate. She complained more and soon felt no gratitude for him at all. Not surprisingly, he soon left the marriage. Sally felt no gratitude for her husband, and soon she had no husband at all.

When you live following The Way, you live with awareness of the gifts in your life and feel gratitude for them.

There are three times every day when you should stop and feel gratitude:

Every morning when you get up, think of 5 things that you are grateful for. You could be thankful for your children, your job, your friends, your talents, even the fact that you simply have another day to live. (There are many sick people in the world who are grateful for every day they are given; you should be too.) As you recall these things, hold that joy in your heart for a few minutes. Feel the inner peace.

Throughout the day, be aware of the little gifts given to you. Perhaps someone let you through a traffic light in the middle of rush hour. Perhaps someone held the door open for you at the store. Perhaps a flower bloomed in your garden. If you go through life being consumed by negativity, it is difficult to notice the small but lovely gifts in life. Instead, as you go through your day be aware of all the little gifts you are given. Feel gratitude for them. Give thanks for them. Feel the inner peace it brings you.

In the evening while lying in bed and winding down from the day, try to recall the best thing that happened to you today. I love this practice because it requires you to think of all the good things that happened, and then pick the very best. Again, as you recall the day, feel joy and gratitude for all you have. Feel the inner peace.

If you do this – feeling gratitude morning, throughout the day, and evening – you are living with gratitude all day long! You are consciously aware of all that you have been blessed this. This brings you inner peace... and more good blessings.

Chapter Four:
Respecting Your Temple

Although your body is a temporary one, it is the one you have for your entire lifetime here on Earth. Made of skin, bones, muscles, nerves, and organs, it is a beautiful piece of human machinery whose functions were designed to work perfectly together to sustain your life. What goes on in your body at any given moment is nothing short of a miracle!

Through DNA, every cell knows its function. If it's a cell within your heart, it helps your heart pump blood to all the other cells of your body. If it's a cell in your skin, it helps your body regulate body temperature, fight potential invading organisms, and heal when cut. Deeper within every cell is the ability to convert fuel (in the form of glucose, protein, etc.) into energy that will keep your muscles moving, your lungs breathing, your brain learning and thinking. All this goes on every second of every day, throughout your whole life.

Is there any question, then, that your body should be respected as the amazing temple it is?

The Body Conflict

Inner conflict often arises when your True Self – the spirit that lives within you -- does not match the body that houses it. In your heart, you know you have a purpose here on Earth. You have dreams of the many accomplishments you want to achieve. You know in your heart – your True Self – that you are here to contribute something big to the world. Is your body going to keep up with your dreams?

When your body is healthy enough to carry out your dreams, you live with inner peace. And, having a healthy body is almost always within your control. (Please note that I completely understand and appreciate that people with physical handicaps or mental disabilities cannot control the circumstances they have been given. However, those with disabilities also have higher purposes that give them fulfillment and inner peace. In fact, it is possible that their disabilities may be actually be part of their spiritual journey here on Earth – something their souls agreed to in order to learn and grow, or help others learn and grow. As such, they should also keep as healthy as they possibly can in order to fulfill their purposes.)

The majority of illnesses and diseases are caused by what you do to your body. Through neglect or through damaging acts such as the overindulgence of food, drugs and alcohol, the body becomes ill. Heart disease, high blood pressure, diabetes, and more, have all been proven to be a result of these external factors that you can control. So if you want to live with inner peace, you must respect your body – your temple – avoid destructive substances, and honor it through appropriate food, movement, and rest.

Food

Becoming a Certified Health Coach through the Institute for Integrative Nutrition® (www.instituteforintegrativenutrition.com) was such an eye-opening experience for me. One of the most important lessons I learned is that what has happened to our food supply as a result of modern technology is nothing short of abominable. Food manufacturers today produce low quality foods, stripped away of most nutrients. In their place, they have added sugar, salt and fat. Packaged foods are everywhere and their convenience continues to make them the go-to foods for most Americans.

Most people live unaware to what has happened to our food sources over the last half century. They assume that if it's sold in a store, then it must be okay. Hardly. Americans today are fatter and sicker than ever before. The abundance of poor quality, factory-manufactured foods has a lot to do with that. When you feed your body sugar, fat, salt, preservatives, additives, etc., it just can't operate as it was intended. When cells and systems are not being fueled properly they can't work properly. You feel sick, you feel tired – and disease occurs.

To live a life of inner peace, living up to your full potential, you need to fuel your body well. That entails eating plenty of unprocessed foods -- foods that come directly from nature, unaltered in a factory. When you fuel your body with fresh vegetables, fruits, whole real grains, legumes, nuts, seeds, meat (if you are not vegetarian) and water (lots and lots of water), your body receives all the nutrients, micronutrients, and hydration it needs to function at top capacity. You'll have energy, you'll have mental focus, you'll have strength, and you'll just plain feel good! Good enough to tackle your daily tasks with energy left over to pursue your dreams.

Movement

If I told you that I loved to exercise I'd be telling you a lie. I really don't. While I know that many people enjoying going to the gym to run on treadmills, take spin classes and lift weights, that doesn't appeal to me in the least. In fact, my home treadmill – as well as ab equipment, thigh machine, and aerobic DVDs – are just dust collector. But, put on a great Bruce Springsteen song and I turn into a dancing fool! Bring me to a hiking trail, and I'm in heaven as I walk through the woods, tackling the switchbacks and reaching the summit.

You see, exercise comes in all forms – and what's right for one person may not be right for another. So don't fret if you don't like to exercise. The secret is to do some physical activity – anything that you enjoy that gets your body moving – so you'll actually do it! My sons love to waterski and run, my step-daughter loves to take Zumba classes, and my husband morphs into a fish when he's near water. So whatever type of physical activity you enjoy, just do it! (as the Nike slogan says) Move your body to keep your body healthy.

Why the need for movement? Moving your body keeps your muscles strong and your joints flexible. It also oxygenates your cells by increasing your circulation. While this is important for your heart and lungs, did you know it's also especial for your brain health and sex health? I'm sure you'd like both of these to function well for as long as possible!

Physical activity (exercise) also produces endorphins and hormones, including mood-elevating serotonin. This is why exercise is such a great stress-reliever and mood enhancer. How much exercise do you need? While there are conflicting reports, here's something to keep in mind: when you move your body long enough to feel your respiration and blood flow increase, your feeling of well-being will also increase.

Metabolism is another reason to move your body. When you partake in cardiovascular and weight resistance exercises, your metabolism increases. This not only burns calories while you are exercising, but your metabolism continues to remain elevated after the exercise, allowing you to make better use of the foods you eat.

Sleep

While food and exercise are synonymous with good health, we often don't think about sleep. Yet this factor is perhaps the most crucial of all, as sleep plays a vital role in your health and well-being.

Time to rest and sleep gives your body an opportunity to recuperate and renew. This is especially important for your brain function, emotional well-being, and your overall physical health.

During sleep, our brains form new pathways for learning the next day. In fact, sleep improves your learning and problem-solving skills. That is why getting enough sleep is so important for children, who are learning so much every day.

In addition to brain health, sleep is crucial for your overall health. During sleep, cells have a chance to repair and rebuild. Lack of sleep is a factor in increased risk of heart disease, kidney disease, high blood pressure, diabetes and stroke. People who lack sleep also have a greater risk of obesity. This is because sleep helps regulate a healthy bala nce of hunger hormones and satiety hormones, as well as the hormone that controls blood sugar.

Sleep also affects your emotions and behaviors. Research has proven that lack of sleep has been linked to stress, mood swings, lack of motivation, depression, and even suicide. This is all medically proven statistics. But on a more metaphysical level, sleep is essential for reviving your spiritual energy, your soul, your True Self – which may also account for low energy conditions like lack of motivation and depression.

When you think about the fact that our souls are energy, it follows that sleep – a time when our physical bodies are unconscious – provides the soul an opportunity to decompress from the physical world and all that happened during the day, and re-energize. Many believe that during sleep your soul can reconnect with the collective energies of Heaven, get messages, evaluate your progress that day, and reorganize your thoughts for the next day. I truly believe this as there are many times when I wake up "knowing" the answers to dilemmas that had me confounded when I went to bed.

Honoring your body means giving it appropriate nourishment, physical activity, and sleep. It means keeping your body as healthy as you can so that you can accomplish all that your spirit inspires. It means resting to give your soul energy a chance to revive. When your body is in harmony with your soul, inner peace can be present.

Chapter Five:
Dealing With Others

Okay, we all have to deal with other people. It's just the way it is. Even monks who vow to silence still have to deal with other monks. Why? Because we need each other. We need each other for security, companionship, belonging, and to advance our souls in this lifetime.

From the time of the cavemen, people needed and depended on each other. Tribes stayed together and moved together. Hunters left the group for days on end, but always returned home to the tribe. In fact, being exiled from the group was a punishment of certain death.

One of the worse feelings a human being can have is to feel isolated from others. Feeling alone contributes to depression, lethargy, and other emotions with low energetic vibration. People (especially teens) who feel isolated from others – even if only in their minds – often resort to destructive thoughts and behaviors. The need for belonging may even cause them to join less-than-savory groups because any sense of belonging is better than aloneness.

This being said, if we have to live with others, we might as well live peacefully with them!

Following The Way, you will find that how you interact with people can affect your inner peace and happiness.

Living with Flexibility

Essential to living with inner peace is the ability to get along with other people. The opposite of getting along is conflict, whether it be physical, emotional or philosophical. Conflict does not equal peace. Conflict does not equal happiness. Conflict equals unrest in your soul and lots of negative energy.

Getting along with others requires you to be flexible. Now I understand that flexibility may not be one of your strongest characteristics, but it should be. Flexibility allows you to see others' viewpoints through empathy – an understanding of their feelings and experiences. Empathy and flexibility go hand-in-hand.

People who are not flexible are very egocentric and limited in their views. It's their way or no way. Well, who died and made them God? With millions of people in the world and many, many cultural and familial differences, why would their way be the only right way?

Today, with the bombardment of mass media and social media, a lot of negative energy is being spread stemming from inflexibility and limited viewpoints. This is a very real problem, as I believe this negative energy is contributing to our growing worldwide discord. It also contributes to your own internal, energetic discord.

.

Debbie had strong social viewpoints. She followed and read many social media pages and tweets that not only promoted her own beliefs but spread hatred about the opposing beliefs. She spent her days – day after day, month after month – consumed in all this negative rhetoric. She felt her blood boiling when she read news that did not coincide with her own beliefs – feeling the hatred right down to her bones. It wasn't long after that she had a freak accident simply walking down the street. Then, she became very ill and had to have surgery. "Why is all this turmoil happening in my life," she thought. Well, it could be because of the negativity that had consumed her life and darkened her spirit.

So, if you're someone who believes that your opinion is the only opinion that everyone should have, and you spread those ideals through negative messages on Facebook, Twitter, or other social media... stop! You're causing a lot of negativity within yourself and bringing the whole world down to boot.

When a person is young, they are soft and tender. When a person dies, they are rigid and stiff.

- Lao Tzu

Living with flexibility allows you to listen to and understand others' feelings, viewpoints, and experiences. You don't have to agree with them, but you can be flexible enough to respect that what's right in one person's mind is not necessarily right in another's. You can agree to disagree, as they say.

Living with flexibility also means that you don't try to control other people – as if they are not their own person, with their own ways of doing things! I am me, and you are you. Who am I to tell you what to think and do?

I am always blown away by parents who try to control their grown children, or spouses who try to control one another. We are all individuals and we were all put here in this world to be our own persons and fulfill our own purposes. We all have free will. Trying to control another person goes directly against that. In addition, when that person doesn't do what you want, the way you want, when you want – you're going to become angry and bitter. This is not the way to inner peace! If you want to find peace and happiness, you have to be flexible and release the need to control others. Concentrate on yourself and focus on your own life.

Living with flexibility, you go through life with a more easygoing attitude. You can hold true to your own beliefs – especially if they strongly resonant with your True Self – but you aren't rigid and unbending. You understand that differences are part of life, and in your heart you are okay with that. If you can get to that point, you will truly find inner peace.

Living with Love and Kindness

In every text that I've ever read about God, it is always said that God is Love – unconditional love. It is always said that one of our life lessons here on Earth is also unconditional love. So if you hope to live in God's likeness, if you hope to eventually pass into an afterlife of love, you must live with love and kindness for others.

My friend Derek, whom I worked with many years ago, had a shirt that read, "Hate is Not a Family Value." I love that message! Derek was a gay man and understood the hatred and bigotry that some people felt toward homosexuality. But is it really our place to judge others? According to the Bible, no.

Let he who has no sin
cast the first stone.

Judging others – whether it be for their gender preference, race, nationality, religion, or any other issue – makes the assumption that you are better than them. Again, who made you God?

Judging others creates discord in your soul -- and that fact really gets to the root of it all. Your Inner Soul came to this life in a pure and loving condition and that is your True Self. It is the experiences in this physical world that create anything less than love.

Living with unconditional love allows you to see beyond yourself. It allows you to interact with others from a place of purity, compassion, and kindness. Everyone deserves to be loved, even by strangers. Have you ever done something kind for someone you don't even know? Holding a door open. Paying for the next person in line at the coffee shop. Sending a greeting card to a soldier abroad. Donating a toy for the local Christmas "adopt a family" program. When you do an act of kindness from a place of love in your heart, your Inner Spirit rejoices.

We are all different – not better, just different. Living with love and kindness – and without judgment – feels really good inside. It creates inner peace.

Living without Drama

I really don't get why some people thrive on chaos and drama. Perhaps they get a rush from turmoil? Perhaps they're hoping to star in a reality television show? I'm not sure. But what I do know is that inner peace and drama cannot co-exist.

Many times, turmoil arises from your own reaction to an event. If someone cuts you off in traffic, you can either get angry and flip him the bird, or you can consider that maybe he's late for work and may lose his job if he doesn't get there on time. Is he right to cut you off, potentially causing an accident? Of course not. But that is not the point. Sometimes sh#t happens in life that you don't like – but how you choose to react is up to you. This is your choice. This is your free will.

Don't let the little annoyances in life become big problems in your mind. Don't let them consume you. Don't let them steal your peace and happiness. There are plenty of important, real issues that you must deal with in life – like a sick child, an aging parent, a failing marriage – so why make a big deal over little things that really don't matter in the larger scope of life? A run in your stockings? Your child spilled his drink? Car needs a repair? Small stuff. Don't sweat it! Keep drama out of your life and your life will be a whole lot happier.

Living without Competition

I truly believe that competition creates greed, and greed creates discord. Yes, competiton prompts us to become better, to challenge ourselves. But when competition turns into greed or pride, or when the prize becomes more important than the challenge endured, competition becomes destructive instead of fulfilling.

Bob wanted to be financially successful in order to provide a secure life for his young family and contribute benevolently to charities he felt closest to his heart. He worked at a fledgling company and helped to turn it into a global corporation. At first, Bob acted out of love and the desire to expand his innate talents and potential. Soon, however, the love of money and power became more of a guiding factor than the love for his family. As he became more successful, rising to higher and higher positions in the company, he began cheating on his wife while away at business conferences. He padded his expense reports to cover overindulgences of alcohol. He bought more and more expensive cars. He bought a house much too large for his needs – not as an investment but as a boastful sign of his material success. He had let healthy competition turn to greed and become negative instead of positive.

Now that is not to say that all competition is bad. It can help you grow in confidence, it can provide the funds needed for living, it can help develop your God-given talents, and so much more. But be watchful for competition that only leads you to be a prisoner to the trappings of the material world – or that creates self-importance over others. Those will not ring true in your heart. Those won't bring you inner peace.

Living with Healthy Boundaries

As mentioned earlier, I believe you should strive for unconditional love towards all. Non-judgmental love. That being said, you also need to have healthy boundaries with others.

You will have contact with many toxic people in this world. And while you can be loving towards them, you don't need to make yourself a victim to their words, beliefs, and behaviors – and you don't need to let them step all over you. Most of these people are innately good – they may even be your family members or friends – but worldly experiences have caused them to develop some negative characteristics, and you don't need to put up with anything that makes you uneasy. These people, whether intentionally or innocently, will disrupt your inner peace.

Negative People

Negative people are everywhere. They are miserable – and let you know about it. They whine and complain about their jobs, families, politics, economics, and just about everything! They lament over the "good 'ol days." They talk negatively about other people. They find fault with everything.

Negativity is quickly and easily spread. It's highly contagious. Have you ever noticed that when one person starts to complain about something, others join in? You'll want to keep your distance from negative people so that their negative energy does not affect your mood or spirit. What if they're your mother, uncle or friend and you really can't distance yourself from them? During a conversation, if talk begins to get negative, you can either change the subject to a new lighter topic, or simply remove yourself from the conversation. Or course, you can also gently confront the person and make them aware of their negative talk (they probably don't even realize they're doing it!). Be careful with this one... it may cause hurt feelings and a lot of family issues!

Abusive People

Abuse comes in many forms. It can be physical, sexual, verbal, emotional or spiritual. It could be the "family friend" who molests a child. It could be the mean girl at school who makes study hall a living hell. It could be a husband who is heavy handed or says demeaning things to his wife. Abusive people don't necessarily know that they're hurting someone. Many times they do, but some times they may not. Many times they become abusive because it's the way they were raised – they learned their behavior from others. That, however, is no reason why you should endure their abuse. Run – don't walk – away from these people!

Controlling People

Earlier we talked about not controlling

others. Well, what if others try to control you? This happens a lot. Parents try to control their children. Spouses try to control one another. Leaders try to control followers.

The first step in dealing with controlling people is to know, love, and trust yourself. What is it that YOU want? What feels right to you? Gather your strength and stand your ground firmly. You don't need to be confrontational with them. Just let them know you have your own thoughts on that subject matter or you want to do something your own way. Do what feels right in your heart and you can't go wrong.

Chapter Six:

You And the World

The Oneness of All

According to work of Albert Einstein, the German physicist and one of the greatest geniuses of our time, everything is energy, and all energy in the universe is connected. Recent studies in quantum physics also prove this theory. This book is made of energy. You are made of energy. In addition, all energy has a frequency or vibration; and when the vibration of one thing changes, it makes a ripple effect throughout the universe.

In the philosophy known as Taoism, as well as in many religions, the world and everything in it is also seen as one complete whole. Everything is interconnected through spirit, and when something happens to one thing, it sets off a chain reaction that reaches far beyond the initial action.

Both science and age-old religions believe that through energy, everything is connected. There is a Oneness of all that exists.

This is very important to know and understand, because it is highly relevant to your life

The Ripple Effect

Since everything is made up of energy, it is important to understand that everything you *think* and *do* has a ripple effect that expands far beyond yourself and into the world. Since thoughts and actions are made of energy, when you have any thought at all – positive or negative – or take any action at all – positive or negative – this energy spreads throughout the universe making alterations to other energies and bringing like energies together.

An example that is easy to understand is how someone's mood can affect yours. Earlier in this book we talked about negativity and how it is very contagious. That's because feelings, thoughts, words, and actions are all made of energy. If you've ever been around someone who's negative or acts rudely towards you, chances are your mood and thoughts turned negative too.

The opposite is also true. The next time you are in a checkout line at a store and the cashier seems grumpy and rude, try to influence her mood into a positive direction. Smile at her and share some kind words. You'll see that your loving positive energy travels right to and through her, helping to make her day better. Plus, she'll then pass that good spirit on to others...the ripple effect!

Now take that momentum to a grander scale. Riots often start from a small negative action that multiplies through a large group, growing ever stronger until it reaches the level of mass anger and hysteria. At the other end of the spectrum, group healings work the same way. Have you ever been part of a prayer group that prays for someone who's ill, and against all odds they are blessed with a quick recovery? Collective energy is very powerful! But it's up to all of us to decide how to use this powerful tool and knowledge.

How will you make a ripple effect in the world? Will you spread negativity by maliciously gossiping about other people? Or, will you spread love by donating food to your local Thanksgiving food drive? Will you spread negativity by ridiculing your child or spouse? Or, will you spread love by babysitting for an over-stressed mother who needs a little time for herself? If you're reading this book, I know you will share your loving energy and help make life better for all.

Law of Attraction

The Law of Attraction uses this same law of energy – where like attracts like. And using it wisely can help you create a blessed life. This law states that the energies of your thoughts and feelings will reach out into the universe and, by attracting the same energies, bring what you desire to you. It is important, then, to be highly aware of what you are thinking and feeling. If you are feeling positive and spreading good vibrations, more good will come to you. But if you are thinking negative thoughts, you will bring more negativity to you.

Take Sam, for instance. He had a really restless sleep one night and woke up in a cranky mood. He just knew it would be a bad day – he had already made up his mind through his thoughts and feelings that it would be bad. Then, sure enough, his expectations came true! He spilled his morning coffee on his shirt, he ran into heavy traffic on the way to work, his computer was acting up, and a contract that he thought was a done-deal fell through. Sam had decided it would be a bad day, and he was right. Or did he attract it to himself?

The Law of Attraction – and using it – is made up of three main steps:

Conceive (think)

Believe (feel)

Receive (manifest)

There are many books that are dedicated specifically to this universal law so I won't go into great depth about the specifics and how you can apply them to get the larger things in life (love, money, success, etc.). But what I will include here is an important lesson I've learned:

Using the Law of Attraction cannot be a half-hearted attempt, because the energy you give out will be weak and will not attract what you desire. The key to successfully using the Law of Attraction is to DECIDE. Decide what you want – not HOPE for, but DECIDE.

Decision and hope are two totally different things. Deciding creates a concrete feeling of definitiveness. If you want something, decide it is yours. Make it a definite. Conceive it in great detail and then believe it and feel it as though it were true. KNOW that it is yours. DECIDE that it is yours.

The Way to inner peace and happiness requires you to understand that you are energy and how you use your energy will affect your life, your peace, and your happiness. Spread positive energy and surround yourself with people who do the same. You cannot find inner peace and happiness when you are attracting negative energies.

Reconnecting with Nature

Whenever I am feeling overwhelmed by life or feel that my soul needs some revitalizing, I head out to nature. Whether I find myself sitting on bench by a stream, or a hiking a trail at my locate park, being outdoors – breathing in fresh air, seeing the mighty examples of God's perfect creations – I find my inner peace again.

Why does nature have that affect on us? I think it's because nature, for the most part, remains the way God created it. Pure and unaffected, the energy in nature is positive and fulfilling to the soul. We feel tranquil and serene inside, and feel harmony with the world.

Pure, clean oxygen in the air. Warmth and light from the sun. Our senses become filled with peace and completeness. Our troubles disappear amongst the grandeur of the world as we become less engrossed in ourselves, and instead, become part of something much bigger than ourselves.

To replenish your soul and find inner peace and happiness, get outdoors and into nature. Find time at least once a week to be outside surrounded by grass, trees, and sky. You will be surprised how amazing this simple act will make you feel.

Living Simply

*"As you simplify your life,
the laws of the universe will be simpler."*
-Henry David Thoreau

We live in a world where everyone is striving for more – more money, more "toys," more real estate, more, more, more. But, having more things are just more things to worry about!

"More" sometimes just clutters up life. Look around your home. How many items do you see that were from years ago? Perhaps someone gave you an item that you really don't like. Perhaps you still have an old piece of furniture from a past relationship? Old items hold a lot of old connotations and emotional attachments. Hanging on to too many old possessions keeps you linked to your past and energetically holds your back from experiencing beautiful moments in the future. Reducing the amount of material distractions in your life will allow you to appreciate the more important spiritual rewards of life. *Less* creates *more* to appreciate.

In the ancient Chinese practice of Feng Shui, it is believed that clutter in an area stagnates the natural energy (chi) in that space. Energy must be allowed to flow freely and accumulated objects – junk mail, old magazines, unfinished projects, etc. – create blockages for that energy. According to the principles of Feng Shui, clearing clutter and improving the flow of energy can bring about increased prosperity, better health, and personal happiness.

Simplifying your life also goes beyond material possessions to include how you live your life. Sometimes you rush through life – too many things to do, too many places to go, too many people to see. What if you just slowed down a bit? Is it really necessary for you and your family to be involved in so many activities? Wouldn't it be healthier (and happier) to spend quality time together, perhaps taking a walk or spending time chatting and reconnecting?

Living simply is all about saying no. No to excessive material possessions that clutter your life. No to too many obligation of your time. No to pulling yourself in too many directions until you can't focus on any. Simplifying your life provides peacefulness to your house, your life and your soul.

Handling Life's Lemons

In the Taoist philosophy, there is a term called "wu wei." Loosely, it means "without doing." It means you "go with the flow" rather than struggle against. One of my favorite lessons in the Taoist religious text, the Tao Te Ching, gives the example of a oak tree, mighty, strong, and imposing. A strong wind storm came and because the oak was rigid and unmoving, it broke. However, a nearby willow tree, gentle and flowing freely with the wind, was able to withstand the storm without damage.

I also like the saying, "When life gives you lemons, make lemonade!"

Trees and lemons? What do these two seemingly different ideas have in common? The lesson here is this: to have inner peace, you have to be flexible enough to withstand all the things that life may throw at you. Soft and peaceful in nature, you don't fight against matters (storms and lemons), but instead work with them to find positive outcomes and resolutions. Being hard and unmoving when you come across conflicts in life will only make you angry, resentful, and negative. But if you go with the flow, you can withstand life's tribulations while keeping your inner peace.

Chapter Seven:

Fulfilling Your Purpose

Each one of us comes to this world with a purpose to fulfill. This purpose might be a lesson to learn to strengthen and grow your soul. Or your purpose could be helping others in the world. Perhaps it is to enlighten others to The Way. Striving to fulfill your purpose brings you inner peace and happiness because it's what you are really about. But how do you know what your purpose is?

Finding Your Purpose

Whatever your purpose may be, chances are that you may never know what it really is until you leave this world and rejoin the Collective Consciousness of the afterlife (God, Heaven). I know this may sound defeating –

I mean, wouldn't we all try to fulfill our purpose if we only knew what that purpose was?

Your True Self, your soul, innately knows what you were sent here into this world to do. It knows the lessons you were meant to learn. It knows the purpose you are meant to serve. But the physical world has a way of cluttering our minds and our lives until it is difficult to see the truth. Your task, then, is to be open to the many signs that come along throughout your life that will point you in the direction of your purpose or life lesson. Through synchronicity, the universe will always provide people, things, and events in your life that will take you in the right direction. But being aware of those things, being open to those things, seeing those things for what they truly are, can be difficult.

You may not immediately recognize when the right people come along who can be a stepping stone to you reaching a goal. But the universe put them in your path. You may not immediately recognize an opportunity that could potentially bring you in a new direction. But the universe put it in your path. You must stay present in the moment to recognize these gifts.

Being acutely aware in the present moment, being open to Spirit in the present moment, allows you to see signs that will help you find and fulfill your purpose. When you are preoccupied with what might have been yesterday or worrying about what might be tomorrow, you cannot be open to receiving the clues that life brings to you today, right now.

Practicing daily meditation is an easy way to be in the present moment and provides an open channel for finding and fulfilling your purpose. When you meditate, you open your self to God and the universe. Through meditation you can receive information or knowledge that will guide you to the right path.

One of my favorite daily morning practices is to quiet my mind and ask God (prayer) for what I need to know now. Then, I sit quietly (meditation) and listen for whatever message comes. This is a beautiful practice that you should also do every day in order to continue on the right path to your purpose.

Living Fully

There are many paths to finding and fulfilling your purpose, but the best way to honor the life that you have been given to fulfill your purpose is to live it to its fullest. Watch for the signs and make the most of every opportunity that comes your way. Know that everything that happens – good or bad – is aligned to help you serve your purpose. Things may not always happen the way you'd like, but even misfortunes carry a lesson and purpose. Recognize them. Appreciate them. Learn from them, and then continue on.

One of the saddest wastes in life is blaming others for misfortunes. If you are someone who does this, stop immediately! Blaming is just an excuse for not living your life fully and for not honoring your True Self. Instead of blaming someone for the way you were treated or for something negative that happened to you, see it for the lesson it taught you and turn it around to create something good and positive.

A perfect example of this is my friend Brian. Brian's dad abandoned his family when he was just a young child. His mother was left to raise him and his brother – and it was very difficult for her. Money was tight. Brian and his brother were left alone while his mother worked. There wasn't much time to play sports or participate in boy scouts, as most of his schoolmates did. But Brian didn't spend his life blaming his father. Instead, he took all the lessons he learned from his circumstances and created the best life he could. He went to college. He got a great job making a lot of money. He married and had two children. And today, Brian loves being a great dad to his two children.

Trust the process of life! Honor it, accept it, and learn from it. Live life fully and in a way that you'll have few regrets. And finally, live your life by following The Way – all that has been taught throughout this book – so that you can live closest to your True Self. By living The Way, your soul – which innately knows your purpose – will help keep you on the right path so that your purpose unfolds naturally and your life is joyful and meaningful. Then, you will know true inner peace and happiness.